It is been ten years because responsive style started to revolutionize the net, and because then it's turn out to be the business regular. The fast increase of cellular searching (and an limitless assortment of gadgets and display measurements) has produced crucial usability problems for conventional web sites. Designers and builders started experimenting with numerous methods to create styles adapt towards the user's gadget as being a one-website-fits-all answer. This laid the groundwork for what would turn out to be referred to as "responsive style."

The concept of altering logos to satisfy exactly the same consumer needs has mostly remained unthinkable... till now.

Businesses happen to be refreshing their logos into contemporary, simplified variations in the last couple of many years and responsive emblem style will be the rational subsequent stage in assembly the needs of these days.

Flat style is evolving, and gradients are creating their modern-day comeback as being a flat style improvement. This improvement is a component of the style update frequently known as "flat two.0" or "semi-flat design". Their reappearance in iOS and adoption by business leaders like Stripe and Instagram have solidified their recognition as soon as once more, and you will be viewing them within the type of lively UI, branding, backgrounds, illustrations and overlays.

As kids from the 80's and 90's turn out to be much more notable and influential as each brand name leaders and important goal audiences, this pattern can include visible pleasure also as being a contact of nostalgia for your styles.

The fast development of Augmented Actuality or 'AR' won't only be observed within the video games, video clip and application business. We think that AR has great prospective customers of using more than the look neighborhood also, especially with cellular gadgets. A possible supply of inspiration might originate from DIA Studio, utilizing interactive 3D typography on daily objects.

New resources (like tablets, stylos, and so on.) and new applications are which makes it easier to make use of hand-drawn methods and merge it with electronic. The times of 'old brushes in Photoshop' are actually formally more than. The brand new pattern, known as 'digital paintbrush', is far much more flexible, using proportions and in the end providing off a far more contemporary and aesthetically satisfying appear. Much more and much more brand names like Adobe or Nike are integrating their brand name or item utilizing this method.

"The new Dropbox brand name path, for instance, is performing this with its inventive utilization of pictures, and company identities like NatWest are shifting to some new and contemporary really feel, utilizing the possible of brighter colors to boost greater conversion prices. In my area, electronic, this improvement might be because of the truth that websites can load quicker and screens on telephones are larger, so it is simpler to perform with pictures."

"Throughout 2017, style continues to be obtaining easier, however richer," states Ottignon. "In a globe exactly where consumer encounter is king, complicated brand name methods get within the method of the content material. Perform overrides superfluous style particulars, and each brand name asset requirements to make its location."

So brand names are striving to streamline their main property, but searching to pack much more which means and distinctiveness into every component, he argues. Frequently this begins using the title.

So far as we are able to inform, modern graphic designers happen to be obsessive about the "art of destroying". Every thing that features splashing, scratching, ripping off, breaking or every other type of ruining the aesthetics of the composition is taken into account contemporary in 2018.

The corrupted picture, i.e. the glitch impact, continues to be 1 from the hottest developments within the electronic globe recently. Evidently, what was as soon as irritating for your spectator has now been changed into a really needed impact.

Clearly, horror film followers happen to be acquainted with this particular 1 for ages. Yr 2018 will be the yr when corrupted pictures consider more than graphic style globe, also

Taking part in with colour channels continues to be extensively well-liked amongst designers. The method enables designers to make fantastic illusional results. A holograph, a hallucination, a distorted reality… all these are extremely influential around the viewer that makes "Color channels" 1 from the leading graphic style developments 2018.

Double publicity continues to be a factor for a number of many years now. Although some designers have place this method apart for some time, we certainly see an increase of double publicity styles which amaze the viewer.

For designers as well as other visible creatives operating within the electronic realm, alter is continuous, and becoming ready for what is coming subsequent is really a should. Whilst the resources we use evolve at any time much more quickly, so do preferences and also the requirements of customers. We requested some specialists and creatives inside a number of disciplines to consider the approaching yr and inform us what developments they're preparing for, anticipating, and thrilled to determine arise.

A BROADER Function FOR UX DESIGNERS

UX has lengthy been a self-discipline that overlaps with and extends into numerous others-and in 2018, UX expert and blogger Nick Babich states the function of UX designers is going to broaden once more: "Being a UX designer in 2018 will probably be much less about 'doing all the things yourself' and much more about 'connecting individuals with each other.' This may place the main focus on collaboration, quick prototyping, and automation in a few actions from the UX procedure that formerly had been guide, like the look handoff."

NEW Systems IN Kind

Adobe Kind Senior Supervisor Dan Rhatigan states that 2018 will see some shifts not always within the typefaces we use, but in how we utilize them: "The possible of what individuals can perform with typefaces is altering fairly markedly for your initial time in about twenty years," he states. "The fundamental technologies is viewing a fairly significant update correct now."

ON AN Extremely VIOLET WAVELENGTH

Pantone has nominated its colour of 2018: states she has currently been viewing the colour utilized in thrilling methods: "It's not only Pantone's colour from the yr; it's been getting recognition throughout 2017, frequently accompanied by scorching pink, vibrant blue, and cyan. There is little doubt we'll see a great deal of graphic style in 2018 exactly where a glowing extremely violet will be the dominant colour." Grønlund carries on, "It's outstanding to determine this colour, which has been certainly one of the minimum well-liked colours in Europe and America-especially disliked by men-getting this kind of a powerful revival. A ecu study lately confirmed that only 3 % of individuals rated it as their preferred colour, but this really is most likely likely to alter within the new yr."

Typography gets to be the protagonist

With dwindling interest spans and data tiredness turning into an actual problem, designers will vacation resort to typography as their indicates of storytelling. Which basically indicates we're likely to see a great deal of remarkable typography in headers and hero pictures. Geometric sans serif appears to be paving way for your beautiful serifs that makes a comeback and dominate the headings. Be ready to see much more of bolder and oddly spaced letter.

Customized artwork and illustrations consider the middle phase

We noticed this 1 blooming in 2017 when using the likes of Medium, Mozilla and Slack overhauled their brand name with plenty of customized illustrations. Devoted artwork not just assists in conveying a tale much better but additionally is available in useful whilst making a particular and distinctive style. What we noticed final yr may just be the suggestion from the iceberg, as 2018 appears just like the yr when customized illustrations consider the limelight in website design and branding.

High-res content material gets to be the necessity from the hour

Producers are pumping pixels within the smallest of screens and customers are pushed to visible content material. This tends to make it crucial to make high-res content material within the type of photos and video clip. Gadgets with infinity shows just like the apple iphone X and Galaxy S8 are creating the consumer encounter much more immersive, that makes all of it the greater essential for an application to supply complete display encounter. Therefore, it'll only be a good idea to utilize all of this pixel energy to provide wealthy imagery to interact the consumer

Video clip carries on to dominate albeit inside a new dimension

We usually noticed this 1 coming. Video clip usage is steadily increasing because 2015. From internet sequence to item explainer movies?-?users' favored option of content material appears to be seriously skewed in the direction of video clip. The arrival of 360° movies and reside movies on platforms like Fb and Instagram are evidence that viewers just cannot get sufficient from the movie. Anticipate much more brand names to make use of this structure to provide prompt info. 2018 may also be the yr of portrait movies as a lot more people selected to eat video clip content material on their own mobiles in portrait structure.

An internet site continues to be the crown jewel of the company's on-line advertising initiative. The number of occasions each day would you say, "Just verify our website" or "We wish to generate individuals towards the web site." It is all-natural simply because that is the location exactly where your tale is. Your previous, your long term. Your goods, your e-commerce. Furthermore, your site is usually open up and signifies you whenever you cannot be bodily current your self.

But is your site performing everything you experienced hoped it might? Could it be exhausted? Could it be practical? Could it be changing guests? Perhaps it just requirements a refresh for your new yr. I have recognized 5 website design developments to kick off 2018 to create certain your website states you are greater than prepared for company.

Animation

For 2018, animation is extremely a lot in. Animation delivers a brand's tale to lifestyle rapidly and it is particularly efficient when drawing guests towards the house web page. It could talk complicated messages effortlessly as well as in methods that viewers can grasp immediately. Animation may also assist portray a brand name as electronic savvy since it shares its tale inside a dynamic way.

Particular animation techniques which will display up in 2018 are animated logos and GIFs. Animating a emblem assists a brand name deliver much more lifestyle to its persona and may be potent and fascinating when executed correctly. The proliferation of style resources with simplified interfaces opens up the execution of animation to higher audiences and much more businesses.

Typography

Although some brand names will ramp up their animation, other people can make typography their instrument for garnering interest and pulling guests in. Typography has usually been current on web sites, but we're referring to fonts with much more character that consider much more visible existence on the web page. Typography may also be ramped up in dimension, taking up the function of other graphics and visuals, basically turning into a visible entity by itself. Some brand names are currently experimenting with typography and utilizing just one font all through the entire website. This differs from previous fashion recommendations, which inspired a minimum of two or 3 various fonts, but some just like the minimalism and ease that utilizing just one font portrays.

Daring Colours

2018 would be the yr of disruption. Utilizing daring, contrasting colours will symbolize what is heading on. The pattern for placing with each other two or even more colours that do not appear suitable will reinforce because the yr extends. New style resources like Khroma are assisting designers experiment and consider dangers they may have shied far from previously. They are sharing daring representations for brand names and displaying the planet that colours have extraordinary psychological influence and therefore are important in telling a brand name tale and capturing its persona.

Various and vibrant colour strategies

Generally, we all know the unwritten rule of dealing with a brand name and social networking style.

Adhere towards the brand name or logo's colours.

Nicely, 2018 will be the yr to go wild simply because brand names are escaping this rule and operating wild and totally free!

Businesses are actually searching for new methods to face out within the social networking landscape, particularly 1 as saturated as ours. Particular businesses are rebranding especially for this objective, and they are rebranding using the rainbow.

Appear at Dropbox, whose 2017 choice to toss absent their 2-solid colour plan has noticed a lot achievement, as well as their new catalog of vibrant and numerous colours.

This new alter enabled Dropbox to widen their creativeness for his or her customer's on-line encounter and for his or her social platforms, with out altering their very well-known emblem.

The brand new brand name colours display Dropbox's development and maturity, heading from the easy on-line storage web site to some location for creatives to share function.

Now, Dropbox is really a colourful and very noticeable existence on the web, having a wide selection of enjoyable and eccentric social networking styles.

The worldwide on-line auction home and vendor, eBay also moved on to brighter colours, making a far more thrilling social networking and web site.

Mesmerizing Gradients

Gradients might have existed for some time, all of the way back again to our elementary times when providing your essay titles a rainbow gradient produced you're feeling tremendous essential and expert, but it is continuing to brighten up dull backgrounds having a vengeance.

Currently creating a well known comeback in 2017, this pattern appears to be developing much more momentum, and will nicely be considered a primary style pattern of 2018.

Designers are likely to have a good time taking part in about with various colour mixtures, and clients are likely to adore it, in the easy 2-colored to gradient meshes with more than five.

For social networking, this pattern is an additional enjoyable and thrilling alter for a lot of businesses, using the exact same advantages as vibrant strong backgrounds.

Double Exposures

This was this kind of a large pattern in 2017, in the newbie designer to high-end professionals, web sites and portfolios had been full of them.

This easy to complete, at time, style method has captivated audiences all of final yr, and also the pattern will only carry on to develop.

Moody Tones

The 80/90s are obviously back again, and also the wild recognition of sequence like Stranger Issues is strong evidence. Together with that period arrives a renewed curiosity in colours that were not perceived as vibrant. For numerous factors, the colours captured by gadgets back again then had been relatively worn out and never as saturated. This phenomenon has impressed numerous designers' choice for moody colour palettes to become utilized with all types of supplies: display, paper, material, amongst numerous other people.

Probably the simplest way to determine this pattern would be to see moody filters utilized to normal pictures:

In colour concept, we make use of the phrase worth to specific that relative brightness or darkness. Moodier tones possess a reduce worth, creating them seem darker. Likewise, there is an additional trait known as Chroma that actions the caliber of a color's depth or purity. Because moody colours are distant from their pure, saturated bases (believe main crimson or blue), they're stated to possess a reduced Chroma.

two. Extremely Violet and Galactic Results

Pantone just named Extremely Violet its Colour from the Yr for 2018. This deep, blue-based purple displays the bigger pattern of drawing inspiration from area. Consequently, Extremely Violet does not just stage to literal motifs like stars and planets, but additionally further feelings like our feeling of discovery. Anticipate space-related aesthetics to affect the graphic, internet, inside, and style style industries particularly.

It isn't just the 80s which are creating a comeback. Mid-century, a phrase utilized to explain the time period approximately in between 1933 and 1965, is definitely turning into a supply of inspiration for internet and print designers. Whilst inside and style style have integrated mid-century contemporary components in waves throughout the previous couple of a long time, now we are observing a far more electronic adoption and interpretation of these components. Just check out a few of the illustration designs and colour palettes in use all around the internet

Colour Fonts

In the event you have not turn out to be acquainted using the idea of colour fonts, you may be lacking out on the important style instrument. We have mentioned why Colour Fonts would be the subsequent large factor in typography, as well as how you can produce your personal font, however it is really in 2018 when this structure will turn out to be extremely well-liked. Why? Since the software program enabling colour font use has only just been launched (I am referring to Photoshop CC 2017/2018 or Illustrator CC 2018). Anticipate to determine numerous much more colour fonts in improvement and use throughout 2018! Meanwhile, right here are a few of our favorites in the market.